Jesus: When God Became A Man

BIBLE STUDY GUIDE

From the Bible-teaching ministry of

Charles R. Swindoll

INSIGHT FOR LIVING

Charles R. Swindoll is a graduate of Dallas Theological Seminary and has served as senior pastor of the First Evangelical Free Church of Fullerton, California, since 1971. Chuck's radio program, "Insight for Living," began in 1979. In addition to his church and radio ministries, Chuck enjoys writing. He has authored numerous books and booklets on a variety of subjects.

Based on the outlines and transcripts of Chuck's sermons, the study guide text is co-authored by Bryce Klabunde, a graduate of Biola University and Dallas Theological Seminary. He also wrote the Living Insights sections.

Editor in Chief:
Cynthia Swindoll

Coauthor of Text:
Bryce Klabunde

Assistant Editor:
Wendy Peterson

Copy Editors:
Deborah Gibbs
Cheryl Gilmore
Karene Wells

Designer:
Gary Lett

Publishing System Specialist:
Bob Haskins

Director, Communications Division:
Deedee Snyder

Manager, Creative Services:
Alene Cooper

Project Supervisor:
Susan Nelson

Print Production Manager:
John Norton

Printer:
Sinclair Printing Company

Unless otherwise identified, all Scripture references are from the New American Standard Bible, © The Lockman Foundation 1960, 1962, 1963, 1968, 1971, 1972, 1973, 1975, 1977. Used by permission. The other translation cited is The Living Bible [LB].

An effort has been made to locate sources and obtain permission where necessary for the quotations used in this book. In the event of any unintentional omission, a modification will gladly be incorporated in future printings.

ISBN 0-8499-8478-5
Printed in the United States of America

COVER DESIGN: Nina Paris
COVER PAINTING: Scala/Art Resource, NY

Contents

INTRODUCTION

No matter what time of year it is, just thinking about Christmas is enough to put a smile on my face. I can see the beautiful colors that seem to dance about the streets. I can smell the pine logs crackling in the fireplace. And the music—there's nothing like it!

And yet, how much do we really know about the songs we sing and verses we read at Christmastime? It's easy to go through the motions of trimming the tree, hanging the lights, and wrapping the presents without really understanding what Christmas is all about.

Whether Christmas is a few days or a few months away, it seems to me we could add substance to our traditions and knowledge to our faith by stepping back and looking deeper into all that surrounded Jesus' birth. For instance, do you know what Jesus was doing before He entered the world as a baby? Why did He come in the first place? What was it like for Him to become human? And what has He been doing since He came? In this study, we'll answer these questions together and peel away some of the myths surrounding Jesus' first Advent.

Are you ready to unwrap your first Christmas present? Here it is on the pages of this study—our gift to you. May these truths be just what you need to help you really celebrate the birthday of the King of Kings on Christmas Day and every day of the year.

Chuck Swindoll

Chuck Swindoll

PUTTING TRUTH INTO ACTION

Knowledge apart from application falls short of God's desire for His children. He wants us to apply what we learn so that we will change and grow. This study guide was prepared with these goals in mind. As you go through the following pages, we hope your desire to discover biblical truth will grow as your understanding of God's Word increases and that you will be encouraged to apply what you've learned.

To assist you in your study, we've included a section called Living Insights at the end of each lesson. These exercises will challenge you to study further and to think of specific ways to put your discoveries into action.

There are many ways to use this guide—in personal devotions, group studies, discussions with friends and family, and Sunday school classes. And, of course, it's an ideal study aid when you're listening to its corresponding "Insight for Living" radio series.

To benefit most from this study guide, we would encourage you to consider it a spiritual journal. That's why we've included space in the Living Insights for recording your thoughts and discoveries. We hope you'll return to those sections often for review and encouragement as you continue to grow in your walk with Christ.

Bryce Klabunde
Coauthor of Text
Author of Living Insights

Jesus: When God Became A Man

Chapter 1

BEFORE THE SON BECAME A BABY

John 1:1–18

In January, the United States celebrates Martin Luther King Jr.'s birthday; in February, George Washington's and Abraham Lincoln's. The birthday celebration of history's most significant person, though, is in December. On the twenty-fifth day of that month, shops shut their doors, families gather together, and people all over the world remember the birth of Jesus of Nazareth.

Think of the many songs written to commemorate and proclaim Jesus' birth—"Silent Night," "O Come, All Ye Faithful," "Away in a Manger," and hundreds of others written throughout the centuries. Each one offers praise for the baby born in a humble manger long ago. For example, here's the refrain from "The Birthday of a King":

> Alleluia! O how the angels sang.
> Alleluia! How it rang!
> And the sky was bright with a holy light,
>   'twas the birthday of a King.[1]

A birthday celebration—that's what Christmas is all about. But is it accurate to say that Jesus has a birthday in the same sense as Martin Luther King Jr., George Washington, Abraham Lincoln, or any other man or woman?

Many people assume that Jesus' existence began like ours, in the womb of His mother. But is that true? Did life begin for Him with that first breath of Judean air? Can a day in December truly mark the beginning of the Son of God?

---

1. William Harold Neidlinger, "The Birthday of a King," in *The Hymnal for Worship and Celebration* (Waco, Tex.: Word Music, 1986), no. 162.

1

Unlike us, Jesus existed before His birth, long before there was air to breathe . . . long before the world was born.

The Son of God in Eternity Past

"In the beginning"—the book of John opens with the same momentous words as Moses' account of the Creation (Gen. 1:1). But the gospel writer transports us back beyond the earth's beginning, beyond when the galaxies were spun into space and mountains and rivers and valleys and vast oceans first etched the face of the earth. He guides us to a time before time, where Christ existed with the Father and the Spirit.

> In the beginning was the Word, and the Word was with God, and the Word was God. (John 1:1)

How do we know this "Word" is Christ? Later in the passage, John unveils His identity:

> And the Word became flesh, and dwelt among us, and we beheld His glory, glory as of the only begotten from the Father, full of grace and truth. (v. 14)

Why did John call Jesus "the Word"? According to commentator William Barclay, this title, *Logos* in Greek, is the name for

> the instrument through which God had made the world . . . the thought of God stamped upon the universe . . . what gave a man reason, the power to think and the power to know . . . the creating and guiding and directing power of God, the power which made the universe and kept it going. . . .
>
> . . . So John went out to Jews and Greeks to tell them that in Jesus Christ this creating, illuminating, controlling, sustaining mind of God had come to earth. He came to tell them that men need no longer guess and grope; all that they had to do was to look at Jesus and see the Mind of God.[2]

Logos has no beginning; rather, He existed "in the beginning"—the realm of the eternal, triune God. "From everlasting to everlasting, Thou art God," the psalmist wrote (Ps. 90:2); or, as A. W. Tozer

---

2. William Barclay, *The Gospel of John*, vol. 1, rev. ed., The Daily Study Bible Series (Philadelphia, Pa.: Westminster Press, 1975), pp. 36–37.

paraphrased it,

> "From the vanishing point to the vanishing point."
> . . . The mind looks backward in time till the dim
> past vanishes, then turns and looks into the future till
> thought and imagination collapse from exhaustion;
> and God is at both points, unaffected by either.[3]

There in eternity past, the Word was *with* God, communing in perfect harmony with the Father and the Spirit (see John 1:2). Yet He also *was* God. Therein is the mystery of the Trinity: the Father, Son, and Holy Spirit—three in one. Coequal, coexistent, and co-eternal.

Further evidence of Jesus' eternal preexistence comes later in John's gospel, first from Jesus' older cousin, John the Baptizer:

- "This was He of whom I said, 'He who comes after me has a higher rank than I, *for He existed before me.*'" (v. 15b, emphasis added)

and then from Christ Himself:

- "I have come down from heaven" (6:38a)

- "Before Abraham was born, I am" (8:58b)

- "Glorify Thou Me together with Thyself, Father, with the glory which I had with Thee before the world was" (17:5)

The Son of God at Creation

What was Jesus doing in eternity past? Verse 3 reveals His role in Creation:

> All things came into being by Him, and apart from
> Him nothing came into being that has come into
> being.[4]

Jesus was Creation's master craftsman. First, He established what

---

3. A. W. Tozer, *The Knowledge of the Holy* (New York, N.Y.: Harper and Row, Publishers, 1961), p. 45.

4. John shifts the main verb from "was" to "came into being," which is significant in light of John the Baptizer's introduction in verse 6: "There came a man"—literally, *came into being a man*—"sent from God, whose name was John." The gospel writer used the same verb as in verse 3, showing that, like us, John the Baptizer came into being at his birth—he had a birthday. Jesus never came into being; at His earthly birth, He merely took on human form.

theologians call the divine decrees: the laws of the universe, the plan of redemption, the dissolution of evil, the end of time. Then He designed the verdant valleys that stretch between soaring mountains, the cascading waterfalls, the velvet-green forests, the vast desert skies. All these things reveal the Son's ingenious touch.

And according to the apostle Paul, they also reveal Christ's sustaining power:

> For by Him all things were created, both in the heavens and on earth, visible and invisible, whether thrones or dominions or rulers or authorities—all things have been created by Him and for Him. And He is before all things, and in Him all things hold together. (Col. 1:16–17)

Here's an amazing thought: the baby that Mary held in her arms was holding the universe in place! The little newborn lips that cooed and cried once formed the dynamic words of creation. Those tiny, clutching fists once flung stars into space and planets into orbit. That infant flesh so fair housed the Almighty God.

The Son of God with Flesh

As an ordinary baby, God had come to earth. Incredibly, only a few shepherds tiptoed in to welcome the King. Maybe everyone else expected a more regal fanfare or was too busy to notice. Maybe, as John writes, they really did not want God to come near:

> He was in the world, and the world was made through Him, and the world did not know Him. He came to His own, and those who were His own did not receive Him. (John 1:10–11)

Verse 11 literally says, "He came to His own things"—His own creation—but "His own ones did not receive Him." His own people, like the innkeeper, turned Him away.

The world is still shutting the door to Him. Our children can act out the Christmas story on stage, we can purchase electric nativity scenes to display on our mantles, we can sing the carols and light the candles, but do we know Him? Is He our Savior? Have we received Him?

> But as many as received Him, to them He gave the right to become children of God, even to those who

believe in His name, who were born not of blood,
nor of the will of the flesh, nor of the will of man,
but of God. (vv. 12–13)

Take another look at that baby in the manger. Don't just notice the dimpled cheeks and curly hair; rather, gaze into His eyes. Can you see what's inside Him?

The Word became flesh, and dwelt among us, and
we beheld His glory, glory as of the only begotten
from the Father, full of grace and truth. (v. 14)

Do you see the child *and* the glory, the infant-God? What you are seeing is the Incarnation—God dressed in diapers.

The proof that this is not some illusion is the wonderful fact that He "dwelt among us."[5] Later in Jesus' life, John and others ate with Him, walked with Him, were taught by Him, lived alongside Him. They all testified He was the Son of God.

John records the results of His incarnation: "we beheld His glory," a possible reference to the transfiguration (see Luke 9:28–36), and through Him we have received grace.

His fulness we have all received, and grace upon
grace. (John 1:16)

And in verse 18, John reveals the final result of the Son's coming:

No man has seen God at any time; the only begotten
God, who is in the bosom of the Father, He has
explained Him.

By explaining the Father, Jesus did what no ordinary man could do—bridge the gulf between us and God. Suffering heartache and pain, Jesus knew what it was like to be human. Reclining "in the bosom of the Father," Jesus intimately knew the Divine. And He interpreted or, literally, "exegeted" the Father through His words and actions so that the world could understand and believe in God.

---

5. *Dwelt* literally means "tabernacled." "This is a latent reference to the tabernacle of Israel in the wilderness. The tabernacle was a temporary place where man could meet with God. It was humble in its external appearance, but inside dwelt the *Shekinah* glory." From the study guide *Exalting Christ . . . the Son of God: A Study of John 1–5,* coauthored by Ken Gire, from the Bible-teaching ministry of Charles R. Swindoll (Fullerton, Calif.: Insight for Living, 1987), p. 13.

The Son of God . . . and Us

A stable. A manger. Some animals, a man, a woman, and a baby—the nativity scene looks the same year after year. This Christmas, try viewing it in a different light. See the baby as John describes Him: "in the beginning," "with God," "God." Imagine Him in the misty, precreation past, thinking of you and planning your redemption. Visualize this same Jesus, who wove your body's intricate patterns, knitting a human garment for Himself. Picture Him experiencing your pain and bearing your sin on the cross. Envision Him one day receiving praise from every corner of creation.

This Baby so fair.

◆

The Maker of the universe
As man for man was made a curse;
The claims of laws which He had made
Unto the uttermost He paid.
His holy fingers made the bough
Where grew the thorns that crowned His brow;
The nails that pierced His hands were mined
In secret places He designed.

He made the forests whence there sprung
The tree on which His body hung;
He died upon a cross of wood,
Yet made the hill on which it stood!
The sky which darkened o'er His head
By Him above the earth was spread;
The sun which hid from Him its face
By His decree was poised in space!

The spear which spilt His precious blood
Was tempered in the fires of God;
The grave in which His form was laid
Was hewn in rocks His hands had made!
The throne on which He now appears
Was His from everlasting years!
But a new glory crowns His brow
And every knee to Him shall bow![6]

---

6. Author unknown.

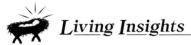 *Living Insights*

Tick. Tick. Tick. Think of the seconds that pass as you read this sentence. There they go, one by one. Whoops, there's another and another; like squirming fish, they slip through your hands. Tick. Tick. Tick. To stop time you would have to stop the earth from rotating. And the stars from burning. And the galaxies from expanding. And . . . well, it's impossible, so don't try.

Time doesn't have a hold on Christ—He created it! He can step in and out of time like a man steps in and out of a river. We float downstream, carried by the steady flow of hours and minutes, but He moves freely and instantly anywhere He wishes. Everywhere we've been and everywhere we'll be, He is there.

> "I am the Alpha and the Omega," says the Lord God, "who is and who was and who is to come, the Almighty." (Rev. 1:8)

Has the passing of time got you worried? Do you feel that time is whisking you into the future before you're ready? What concerns you the most about the future?

_____

_____

_____

Long ago, the Son of God dove headfirst into time and floated along with us for about thirty-three years. As God and man, He offers us both an eternal perspective and a sympathetic understanding of life's voyage. Take a look at Matthew 6:25–34. What reassurances does God give you about your future?

_____

_____

_____

_____

All of time, from the beginning to the end, is in Jesus' hands. Rest in His power.

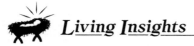

Living Insights

Among the crates of tangled lights and tinsel, the box containing the family's most precious Christmas decoration is the one labeled Nativity Scene. This is the one box the kids let Mom open. Carefully unwrapping each figure, she places them in the exact spot they stood the year before. The shepherds, the angels, the animals, Joseph, and Mary—oblivious to the "Fa la la" of Christmas, they stand poised in perpetual awe of the sleeping baby.

To help draw you into the nativity scene alongside the worshiping figures, we've designed one Living Insight in each chapter of our guide to be an opportunity for adoration. We encourage you to push aside all the distractions and gaze with the angels into the eyes of Jesus.

Let's begin by focusing on Christ's preexistence. What do the following verses tell you about God's eternal nature? By implication, what do they teach you about the nature of the baby Jesus?

Psalm 93:1–2 _____

_____

_____

Isaiah 40:28 _____

_____

_____

The writer to the Hebrews quoted from two psalms that refer directly to Christ (Pss. 45 and 102). What do his quotes tell you about the Son's eternal nature?

Hebrews 1:8–12 _____

_____

_____

Imagine the Creator-God tightly wrapped in swaddling clothes. If you had been there to see Him, what would you have said to glorify Him? What would you have done? As in a journal, write out your words and actions.

Chapter 2

WHY IN HEAVEN WOULD GOD COME DOWN?

Selected Scriptures

When the Son of God was on His throne in heaven, the angels cried "Holy!" and the choirs sang "Gloria!" Pure light radiated from His shimmering garments. Like diamonds, His eyes shone; like thunder, His voice rumbled. On His fingertips, lightning danced.

Then He left His home and entered the womb of a teenage girl. And when the time came, she gave birth to Him on the dirty floor of an animal stall and laid Him in a feeding trough. Because—it's embarrassing to say—there was no room for the Son of God anywhere else on earth.

Max Lucado elaborates on Jesus' inglorious birth.

> God had come near.
>
> He came, not as a flash of light or as an unapproachable conquerer, but as one whose first cries were heard by a peasant girl and a sleepy carpenter. The hands that first held him were unmanicured, calloused, and dirty.
>
> No silk. No ivory. No hype. No party. No hoopla.
>
> Were it not for the shepherds, there would have been no reception. And were it not for a group of stargazers, there would have been no gifts.
>
> Angels watched as Mary changed God's diaper. The universe watched with wonder as The Almighty learned to walk. Children played in the street with him. And had the synagogue leader in Nazareth known who was listening to his sermons . . .
>
> Jesus may have had pimples. He may have been tone-deaf. Perhaps a girl down the street had a crush on him or vice-versa. It could be that his knees were bony. One thing's for sure: He was, while completely divine, completely human.[1]

1. Max Lucado, *God Came Near* (Portland, Oreg.: Multnomah Press, 1987), p. 26.

10

The question is: Why would the Son of God want to become human? Why would He leave His celestial home to enter our world of pain and sorrow? Why would He forsake the worship of angels to be spat upon by hateful people? Why in heaven would God come down?

The reason has to do with a special plan God had formulated long before the first Christmas—a plan whose beginnings can be found on the scrolled pages of the Old Testament.

The Historical Record: Where It Started

We can trace God's plan all the way back to an event in the book of Exodus. The villain in this story is not the paranoid Herod, who slaughters the babies in Bethlehem, but an Egyptian pharaoh who cracks his whip of slavery. Rather than Joseph and Mary, the heroes are Moses and Aaron. And in place of shepherds are the Hebrew people. Although the names and events differ in the two stories, the central theme is the same: deliverance.

Having migrated to Egypt four centuries earlier, the Hebrew people had become a nation of slaves. Their backs and spirits broken, they cried out to the Lord, who sent Moses and Aaron to set them free. "Thus says the Lord, the God of Israel, 'Let My people go,'" the two men announced to Pharaoh. But he refused, so the Lord sent a series of plagues on the Egyptians—plagues designed to change his heart and mind. They worked momentarily, but as soon as each plague ended, Pharaoh still refused to let the people go (Exod. 5:1–10:29).

The Lord then formulated one last plague that would surely dissolve Pharaoh's obstinacy:

> "'I will go through the land of Egypt on that night,
> and will strike down all the first-born in the land of
> Egypt, both man and beast; and against all the gods
> of Egypt I will execute judgments—I am the Lord.'"
> (12:12)

In order for the Hebrews' firstborn to be spared, God gave Moses specific instructions for the people: Each family had to select an unblemished one-year-old lamb and kill it at twilight on the fourteenth day of the Hebrew month Nisan. They had to smear some of the blood on the doorposts of their houses. Then they were to roast the lamb and eat it with unleavened bread and bitter herbs (see vv. 3–8). And one more thing, they needed to "eat it in haste"

(v. 11), because when the Lord struck down the firstborn of Egypt that night, Pharaoh would be in a hurry to release the Hebrews.

God called the meal the Passover, because

> "'the blood shall be a sign for you on the houses where you live; and when I see the blood I will pass over you, and no plague will befall you to destroy you when I strike the land of Egypt.'" (v. 13)

Don't let the familiarity of this story dull its impact—God is a master teacher, and this is one of His finest object lessons. The Lord could have chosen any number of ways to deliver the Hebrews: He could have issued them razor-sharp swords, He could have provided boats for them to escape across the Nile, or He could have wiped out the Egyptian army with a word. Instead, He was teaching His people a never-to-be-forgotten lesson—deliverance from judgment comes through the blood of a pure lamb.

When the fourteenth day of the month arrived, the Hebrews killed the lambs, smeared the blood, and ate their meals in haste. Then,

> it came about at midnight that the Lord struck all the first-born in the land of Egypt, from the first-born of Pharaoh who sat on his throne to the first-born of the captive who was in the dungeon, and all the first-born of cattle. And Pharaoh arose in the night, he and all his servants and all the Egyptians; and there was a great cry in Egypt, for there was no home where there was not someone dead. (vv. 29–30)

As anticipated, the devastated Pharaoh immediately sent away the Hebrews, who left quickly with the Egyptians' gifts of clothing, silver, and gold (vv. 31–36).

These plundered riches later supplied the materials for the tabernacle—the portable center of worship the Hebrews carried with them through the wilderness. When they reached Mount Sinai, God instructed Moses as to how the people should approach Him in the tabernacle, and Moses wrote these regulations in the book of Leviticus. In this handbook, God emphasized the significance of blood:

> "'For the life of the flesh is in the blood, and I have given it to you on the altar to make atonement for

your souls; for it is the blood by reason of the life that makes atonement.'" (Lev. 17:11)

Not only did the Israelites need blood as a sign for God to let His judgment pass over them, but they also needed ongoing blood sacrifices to atone for their sins—to make them *at one* with God again. God requires blood, instead of something else, for the atoning of sin because blood contains life—the life of the sacrifice. The sinless substitute dies so the sinner might be forgiven and live. This is the method of atonement God chose, anticipating the once-and-for-all sacrifice of the coming Lamb of God, the Messiah.

The Prophetic Promise: How It Unfolded

Centuries after the Exodus, God summoned prophets onto Israel's windswept landscape to peer into the spiritual horizon and foretell the characteristics of the future Messiah. According to Isaiah,

> The people who walk in darkness
> Will see a great light;
> Those who live in a dark land,
> The light will shine on them. . . .
> For a child will be born to us, a son will be given
> to us;[2]
> And the government will rest on His shoulders;
> And His name will be called Wonderful Counselor,
> Mighty God,
> Eternal Father, Prince of Peace.
> There will be no end to the increase of His govern-
> ment or of peace,
> On the throne of David and over his kingdom,
> To establish it and to uphold it with justice and
> righteousness
> From then on and forevermore.
> The zeal of the Lord of hosts will accomplish this.
> (9:2, 6–7)

Gazing deeper into the misty future, the seer reveals more of the

---

2. From our historical perch, we can look back and see what Isaiah meant when he said, "a child will be born . . . a son will be given." Horizontally, from Mary the Christ child was born; vertically, from the Father the Son was given. Humanity and deity intermingled in one person, Jesus.

Messiah's character and future reign of righteousness, deliverance, and hope.

> Then a shoot will spring from the stem of Jesse,
> And a branch from his roots will bear fruit.
> And the Spirit of the Lord will rest on Him,
> The spirit of wisdom and understanding,
> The spirit of counsel and strength,
> The spirit of knowledge and the fear of the Lord.
> And He will delight in the fear of the Lord,
> And He will not judge by what His eyes see,
> Nor make a decision by what His ears hear;
> But with righteousness He will judge the poor,
> And decide with fairness for the afflicted of the
>   earth;
> And He will strike the earth with the rod of His
>   mouth,
> And with the breath of His lips He will slay the
>   wicked.
> Also righteousness will be the belt about His loins,
> And faithfulness the belt about His waist.
> (11:1–5)

Such a righteous and regal King—surely He will be born into Jerusalem royalty. But according to the prophet Micah,

> "As for you, Bethlehem Ephrathah,
> Too little to be among the clans of Judah,
> From you One will go forth for Me to be ruler in
>   Israel.
> His goings forth are from long ago,
> From the days of eternity." (5:2)

A humbly born King, a righteous Judge, a sacrificial Lamb— these Old Testament themes and prophecies stir within the reader feelings of hopeful expectation. And when the doors of the New Testament finally swing open, ushering us in to meet the all-in-one Messiah is John the Baptizer.

The Forerunner's Message: What It Included

> There came a man, sent from God, whose name was John. He came for a witness, that he might bear

witness of the light, that all might believe through him. . . .

And this is the witness of John, when the Jews sent to him priests and Levites from Jerusalem to ask him, "Who are you?" . . . He said, "I am a voice of one crying in the wilderness, 'Make straight the way of the Lord,' as Isaiah the prophet said." Now they had been sent from the Pharisees. And they asked him, and said to him, "Why then are you baptizing, if you are not the Christ, nor Elijah, nor the Prophet?" John answered them saying, "I baptize in water, but among you stands One whom you do not know. It is He who comes after me, the thong of whose sandal I am not worthy to untie." These things took place in Bethany beyond the Jordan, where John was baptizing.

The next day he saw Jesus coming to him, and said, "Behold, the Lamb of God who takes away the sin of the world!" (John 1:6–7, 19, 23–29)

John's pronouncement is like a bright red ribbon woven from centuries of Passover celebrations and prophetic anticipations and tied around the heaven-wrapped package of Christ. Jesus is the Lamb of God, whose blood marks the doorposts of our hearts. At the coming judgment, God will pass over us, like He passed over the Hebrew families in Egypt, and lead us into the celestial Promised Land.

Christ is not just the Passover Lamb; He is also our sacrificial Lamb, slain on the heavenly altar and obtaining for us eternal redemption.

For if the blood of goats and bulls and the ashes of a heifer sprinkling those who have been defiled, sanctify for the cleansing of the flesh, how much more will the blood of Christ, who through the eternal Spirit offered Himself without blemish to God, cleanse your conscience from dead works to serve the living God? (Heb. 9:13–14)

Why in heaven would the Son of God come down? This verse provides the answer. He came not to show off His perfection nor to make our lives more comfortable but to offer Himself to God as our sacrificial substitute. The Lamb of God was born to die.

The Practical Meaning: Why He Departed

With a crown of thorns crushed on His brow, spikes hammered through His wrists and feet, and a spear thrust in His side, the Lamb of God was slain on the altar of a rough wooden cross. Why? Because deliverance comes through the blood of a pure lamb. Through the blood, God's wrath toward sin was satisfied—propitiated—once and for all.

> If anyone sins, we have an Advocate with the Father, Jesus Christ the righteous; and He Himself is the propitiation for our sins; and not for ours only, but also for those of the whole world. (1 John 2:1b–2)

Christ the Lamb has secured our deliverance and offers it to each one of us as a Christmas gift, placed with love under a cross-shaped tree.

———◆———

The Dear Bargain

Lord, what is man? why should he cost thee
So dear? what had his ruin lost thee?
Lord, what is man? that thou hast overbought
So much a thing of naught?

What if my faithless soul and I
Would needs fall in
With guilt and sin,
What did the lamb, that he should die?
What did the lamb, that he should need,
When the wolf sins, himself to bleed?

If my base lust,
Bargain'd with death and well-beseeming dust
Why would the white
Lamb's bosom write
The purple name
Of my sin's shame?

Why should his unstain'd breast make good
My blushes with his own heart-blood?

16

O my Saviour, make me see
How dearly thou hast paid for me

That lost again my life may prove
As then in death, so now in love.[3]

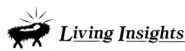 **Living Insights**

In many ways, Jesus' blood was no different than ours. It coursed through His veins just like ours, and it, too, flowed crimson when He pricked His finger. Yet we sing,

There is pow'r, pow'r, wonder-working pow'r
In the blood of the Lamb;
There is pow'r, pow'r, wonder-working pow'r
In the precious blood of the Lamb.[4]

What power does Christ's blood have that ours doesn't? Let's probe a few verses to discover the mighty things it does. After each reference, jot down your findings.

Matthew 26:28 _____

Romans 5:9 _____

Ephesians 2:11–13 _____

Colossians 1:19–20 _____

Hebrews 10:19–22 _____

Hebrews 13:12 _____

1 Peter 1:17–19 _____

1 John 1:6–7 _____

Revelation 1:5 _____

3. Richard Crashaw, from "Charitas Nimia," or "The Dear Bargain," in *Masterpieces of Religious Verse*, ed. James Dalton Morrison (New York, N.Y.: Harper and Brothers Publishers, 1948), no. 697.

4. Lewis E. Jones, "There Is Power in the Blood," in *The Hymnal for Worship and Celebration* (Waco, Tex.: Word Music, 1986), no. 191.

How could His blood accomplish so much? Certainly, if we had been nailed to His cross, there would have been no peace or forgiveness offered anyone. The difference is that His blood represented His sinlessness and His divine love—the love that led Him from heaven to Calvary and into our hearts.

So the next time you prick your finger, think of Christ's blood that He shed for you and the love that once flowed crimson, a long time ago.

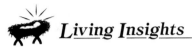 **_Living Insights_**

Have we become accustomed to the Cross? With bowed heads we pass the Communion elements and hear the pastor pronounce the same words and recount the same story. Perhaps it has become like a dear uncle's yarn that always begins, "Have I ever told you about the time I fought alongside 'Old Blood and Guts' Patton in WW II?" "Yes, Uncle," we yawn, but he repeats the story anyway. His story didn't used to make us sleepy. When we were children, we could listen to it again and again.

We encourage you to become a child again as you meditate on the Passion story in Luke 22 and 23. It begins, fittingly, with the Passover the night before Christ the Lamb was slain. Luke's account of the events leading to the Cross is detailed, so take your time and read slowly. Feel it as if it were the first time you've heard it. Afterward, read the following poem and write your own prayer in the space provided, asking the Lord to touch your heart with the power of the Cross.

Good Friday

Am I a stone, and not a sheep,
    That I can stand, O Christ, beneath Thy cross,
    To number drop by drop Thy Blood's slow loss,
And yet not weep?

Not so those women loved
    Who with exceeding grief lamented Thee;
    Not so fallen Peter weeping bitterly;
Not so the thief was moved;

Not so the Sun and Moon
    Which hid their faces in a starless sky.

A horror of great darkness at broad noon—
I, only I.

Yet give not o'er
But seek Thy sheep, true Shepherd of the flock;
Greater than Moses, turn and look once more
And smite a rock.[5]

Commemoration

_____

_____

_____

_____

_____

_____

_____

_____

5. Christina Rossetti, "Good Friday," in *Masterpieces of Religious Verse*, no. 585.

Chapter 3

THE GIFT TOO WONDERFUL FOR WORDS

Philippians 2:5–8

In the Christian story God descends to re-ascend.
He comes down; down from the heights of absolute being
into time and space, down into humanity; . . . down
to the very roots and sea-bed of the Nature He has
created. But He goes down to come up again and bring
the whole ruined world up with Him.[1]

The world's most significant news seldom makes the headlines. For example, about two centuries ago,

> men were following with bated breath the march of
> Napoleon and waiting with feverish impatience for
> the latest news of the wars. And all the while in
> their own homes babies were being born. But who
> could think about "babies"? Everybody was thinking
> about "battles." In one year [1809] lying midway
> between Trafalgar and Waterloo there stole into the
> world a host of heroes! During that one year Glad-
> stone was born in Liverpool, Alfred Tennyson was
> born at the Somersby Rectory, and Oliver Wendell
> Holmes made his first appearance in Massachusetts.
> On the very day of that selfsame year Charles Dar-
> win made his debut at Shrewsbury, and Abraham
> Lincoln drew his first breath in Old Kentucky.[2]

The armies of Napoleon may march across the pages of our history books, but it's the ideas of Darwin and Lincoln and the eloquence of Holmes and Tennyson that have shaped our world. The clamorings of war that seemed so significant then are silent

---

1. C. S. Lewis, *Miracles: A Preliminary Study* (New York, N.Y.: Macmillan Publishing Co., 1960), p. 111.

2. Frank W. Boreham, "Christmas," in *2500 Best Modern Illustrations*, ed. G. B. F. Hallock (New York, N.Y.: Harper and Brothers Publishers, 1935), no. 411.

now, while the infant cries that went unnoticed have heralded our modern times. How the roles have reversed!

If we go back eighteen more centuries, we find the same is true. The shadow of Augustus Caesar's empire loomed large across the Mediterranean world; and when he ordered a census to raise taxes, the news made front-page headlines in every hamlet and town from Europe to the Middle East. But who would have thought that the great Augustus was merely God's errand boy for fulfilling Old Testament prophecy? Who would have noticed the young couple traveling from Nazareth to Bethlehem? And who would have noticed the first cries of newborn Jesus? Who would have cared?

All eyes may have been focused on Caesar and Rome, but the most significant news event of all time had occurred in Bethlehem: the Son of God was born.

Several Scriptures That Provide the Setting

Within the blaring anthems of the world's pomp and power were the subtle, infinite strains of God's omniscient purpose. Let's listen closely to the carefully orchestrated prelude to Christ's birth.

Generally

The apostle Paul noted how God harmonized Old Testament themes with contemporary events.

> When the fulness of the time came, God sent forth
> His Son, born of a woman, born under the Law.
> (Gal. 4:4)

By "the fulness of the time," Paul meant that the conditions were just right for the Son to enter the world. Alexander the Great's career had created the common Greek trade language *Koine*, making it possible years later for people to understand the message of Christ. The elaborate Roman road system also had unwittingly facilitated the rapid movement of the gospel. And the far-reaching census of Caesar prompted Joseph and Mary's trip to Bethlehem so that Jesus' birth would fulfill Micah's prophecy (see 5:2).

Jesus' genealogy is another theme God subtly blends into His nativity overture. In the opening chapter of Matthew's gospel we read:

> And to Jacob was born Joseph the husband of Mary,
> by whom was born Jesus, who is called Christ. (v. 16)

Notice that Matthew does not say "to Joseph was born Jesus." His wording indicates that Jesus was Mary's biological son. The relative pronoun *whom* is feminine and singular: "by *Mary*, Jesus was born." Then who was Jesus' father? Matthew provides the answer in his intimate account of Joseph's discovery of his fiancée's pregnancy.

> When [Jesus'] mother Mary had been betrothed to Joseph, before they came together she was found to be with child by the Holy Spirit. And Joseph her husband, being a righteous man, and not wanting to disgrace her, desired to put her away secretly. But when he had considered this, behold, an angel of the Lord appeared to him in a dream, saying, "Joseph, son of David, do not be afraid to take Mary as your wife; for that which has been conceived in her is of the Holy Spirit. And she will bear a Son; and you shall call His name Jesus, for it is He who will save His people from their sins." Now all this took place that what was spoken by the Lord through the prophet might be fulfilled, saying, "Behold, the virgin shall be with child, and shall bear a Son, and they shall call His name Immanuel," which translated means, "God with us." (vv. 18–23)

The angel could have written this across the sky in thunderous bolts of lightning, but God sent him to Joseph privately in a dream. That's how God often unfolds His plan, discreetly and behind the scenes.

> And Joseph arose from his sleep, and did as the angel of the Lord commanded him, and took her as his wife, and kept her a virgin until she gave birth to a Son; and he called His name Jesus. (vv. 24–25)

Commentator Louis Barbieri helps us understand Joseph's honorable actions in light of first-century Hebrew marriage customs:

> Marriages were arranged for individuals by parents, and contracts were negotiated. After this was accomplished, the individuals were considered married and were called husband and wife. They did not, however, begin to live together. Instead, the woman

continued to live with her parents and the man with his for one year. The waiting period was to demonstrate the faithfulness of the pledge of purity given concerning the bride. If she was found to be with child in this period, she obviously was not pure. . . . Therefore the marriage could be annulled. If, however, the one-year waiting period demonstrated the purity of the bride, the husband would then go to the house of the bride's parents and in a grand processional march lead his bride back to his home. There they would begin to live together as husband and wife and consummate their marriage physically.[3]

Although Joseph was considered Mary's husband during the betrothal period, he was not officially married to her. He had planned "to put her away secretly" or quietly annul the engagement in order to save Mary the public humiliation of being deemed impure. However, seeing God's hand on Mary's virgin womb, Joseph went ahead with his plans to marry her but did not consummate the marriage until after Jesus was born.

The political atmosphere, the prophecies, and the private visions—these strains synchronize and crescendo to the climactic moment when Jesus is born.

Specifically

Now it came about in those days that a decree went out from Caesar Augustus, that a census be taken of all the inhabited earth. This was the first census taken while Quirinius was governor of Syria. And all were proceeding to register for the census, everyone to his own city. And Joseph also went up from Galilee, from the city of Nazareth, to Judea, to the city of David, which is called Bethlehem, because he was of the house and family of David, in order to register, along with Mary, who was engaged to him, and was with child. And it came about that while they were there, the days were completed for

3. Louis A. Barbieri, Jr., "Matthew," in *The Bible Knowledge Commentary*, New Testament ed., ed. John F. Walvoord and Roy B. Zuck (Wheaton, Ill.: Scripture Press Publications, Victor Books, 1983), p. 20.

her to give birth. And she gave birth to her first-born son; and she wrapped Him in cloths, and laid Him in a manger, because there was no room for them in the inn. (Luke 2:1–7)

We can be sure that the newborn son of Caesar would have been laid on silk, and there would have been parades and banners and blaring horns. Only bleating sheep and braying donkeys welcomed God's Son, who lay wrapped in strips of cloth on a pile of hay. Parades and banners? Except for some shepherds and, later, a group of eastern mystics, no one even noticed His birth.

The next morning, the amber sun awoke the village as it always had, women carried their pots to the well, men loaded their mules, children laughed in the streets—it was just another day. But in a stable, the Son of God nestled in His mother's arms, and an awestruck husband silently gazed at his young wife and her nursing child.

Could this helpless infant really be God?

Crucial Statement That Explains the Event

Over the centuries, the mystery of the Incarnation has given theologians plenty of questions to stroke their beards about. How could God descend into the pool of humanity without contaminating Himself with sin? Can God truly remain God—omniscient, omnipresent, and omnipotent—and limit Himself to a man's body? How can Jesus be fully divine *and* fully human?

In Philippians 2:5–8, the apostle Paul offers us some clues toward solving this puzzle.

Before He Actually Came as a Baby

Christ's incarnation began with a humble attitude, which Paul says should infuse our lives as well:

> Have this attitude in yourselves which was also in Christ Jesus, who, although He existed in the form of God, did not regard equality with God a thing to be grasped, but emptied Himself. (vv. 5–7a)

Christ had all the attributes of deity. It is not that He was similar to God; rather, in every form and in every way He was God.[4] The

4. See also John 1:1; 14:9; Colossians 1:19; 2:9; and Hebrews 1:3.

Father, Son, and Holy Spirit lived together in perfect union—coequal, coeternal, and coexistent. Yet He didn't cling to His divine attributes, fighting to hold on to His rights. Instead, He "emptied Himself." He willingly set aside the voluntary use of His divine attributes.

He did *not* set aside His deity but the *voluntary use* of His characteristics as God. At any moment He could have drawn upon any power or prerogative. But in one of the earliest glimmers of grace, He willingly chose to submit Himself to the will of the Father, who had called Him to fill a special earthly role.

When Jesus Actually Arrived

Paul's next three phrases describe that role:

> "taking the form of a bondservant" (v. 7b)
> "being made in the likeness of men" (v. 7c)
> "being found in appearance as a man" (v. 8a)

Existing in the form of God, Christ took on the form of a man, even a slave.[5] As a result, His appearance changed. He no longer looked like God; He looked human and felt human in every way. He hurt, He laughed, and He bled. No halo hovered beatifically over Jesus' head, no royal robes draped His shoulders, no angelic wings graced His back. Because He was human, people could come near Him. Fishermen felt comfortable in His presence. Prostitutes spoke to Him without shrinking back in shame. Even lepers called Him friend.

"He was the God-man," wrote commentator G. Campbell Morgan.

> Not God indwelling a man. Of such there have been many. Not a man Deified. Of such there have been none save in the myths of pagan systems of thought; but God and man, combining in one Personality the two natures, a perpetual enigma and mystery, baffling the possibility of explanation.[6]

---

5. What would it have been like for infinite God to take on a human body? "The Eternal Being," wrote C. S. Lewis, "who knows everything and who created the whole universe, became not only a man but (before that) a baby, and before that a [fetus] inside a Woman's body. If you want to get the hang of it, think how you would like to become a slug or a crab." *Mere Christianity*, rev. ed. (New York, N.Y.: Macmillan Publishing Co., Collier Books, 1952), p. 155.

6. G. Campbell Morgan, *The Crises of the Christ* (Old Tappan, N.J.: Fleming H. Revell Co., 1936), p. 79.

Although we may never completely solve the Incarnation puzzle, that does not stop us from receiving its benefits. Most important for us is that the Son of God did come—"He that made man was made man."[7] And on that fact hangs our life.

Why He Came

Christ came at the Father's bidding to release us from the death-grip of sin. How He accomplished this is the story of the Cross.

> He humbled Himself by becoming obedient to the
> point of death, even death on a cross. (v. 8b)

Can it be—God's Son treated like a criminal? The Judge of humanity judged by humanity, found guilty, sentenced, and executed? What horror! Yet that was the path the Father chose for Him, and He obeyed. Now through Him, God could trade our sin for His righteousness:

> He made Him who knew no sin to be sin on our
> behalf, that we might become the righteousness of
> God in Him. (2 Cor. 5:21)

From the throne room to the manger to the cross, Christ came so that in Him we might pass from bondage to freedom, from death to life.

> Thank God for his Son—his Gift too wonderful
> for words. (9:15 LB)

Underlying Principles That Clarify the Celebration

At Christmastime, thoughts of family, goodwill, and peace on earth fill our minds. But as we ponder the deeper meaning of Christmas—the Christ child, the Incarnation, and the Cross—several truths ring out like the bells on Christmas Eve.

First, *God can do anything.* If He can shape history and move the mind of Caesar, stir life in the womb of a virgin and squeeze Himself into an infant's body, then imagine the great things He can do in our lives.

Second, *God can change anyone.* Through His Son's death on

---

7. C. H. Spurgeon, *Spurgeon at His Best*, comp. Tom Carter (Grand Rapids, Mich.: Baker Book House, 1988), p. 107.

the cross, He changed death into life. What changes can He not perform in our lives?

Third, *God can lead anywhere*. He led Christ from heaven to the cross and back again. Through our valleys, He can lead us as well.

◆

All praise to Thee, Eternal Lord,
  Clothed in a garb of flesh and blood;
Choosing a manger for a throne,
  While worlds on worlds are Thine alone.[8]

 Living Insights

The Son of God's process of "emptying Himself" models a pattern that is central to Christianity: descent and ascent, death and rebirth, surrender and victory. According to C. S. Lewis, this pattern is

> written all over the world. It is the pattern of all vegetable life. It must belittle itself into something hard, small and deathlike, it must fall into the ground: thence the new life re-ascends. . . . So it is also in our moral and emotional life. The first innocent and spontaneous desires have to submit to the deathlike process of control or total denial: but from that there is a re-ascent to fully formed character in which the strength of the original material all operates but in a new way. Death and Re-birth— go down to go up—it is a key principle. Through this bottleneck, this belittlement, the highroad nearly always lies.[9]

Take a moment to read John 12:24–26 and write down the different ways Jesus expresses this principle.

---

8. Martin Luther, as quoted by J. Oswald Sanders in *The Incomparable Christ*, rev. and enl. (Chicago, Ill.: Moody Press, 1971), p. 12.

9. Lewis, *Miracles*, p. 112.

Dying to self through surrender and servanthood makes little sense in a day when seemingly everyone else is busy climbing their ladders to success. But if we truly desire greatness in the Father's eyes, the way up is down.

Let's consider how this concept works itself out in our lives. Suppose a friend makes a bold statement you know is incorrect. Naturally, your first response is to debate the point and prove that he or she is wrong. This boosts your feelings of importance but shames your friend. What do you think would be a more humble approach?

_____

_____

_____

Here's another example. Your spouse is upset because you've been neglecting some of your obligations. Your first response is to make excuses and list alibis. What would be a more servant-hearted way to handle your spouse's complaints?

_____

_____

_____

The Incarnation was not just a one-time event we look back on with gratitude. It was meant to be repeated in little ways over and over in our lives. Use the remaining space to describe a situation in your life in which you can express Christ's self-emptying attitude and how you plan to live it out.

_____

_____

_____

_____

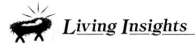 *Living Insights*

Let's allow this sound advice from Warren Wiersbe to guide us into a time of worship.

> There is today such an emphasis on Bible knowledge that we are in danger of ignoring, or even opposing, personal spiritual experience. While we must not base our theology on experience, neither must we debase our theology by divorcing it from experience. If true worship is the response of the *whole* person to God, then we dare not neglect the emotions. We permit people to express their emotions at weddings, funerals, and athletic events, but not at a worship service. The important thing today seems to be that you mark your Bible and write outlines in your note-book, but whatever else you do, keep your emotions hidden! [10]

Take a few moments to allow the truth of the Incarnation to sink into your heart. Don't hide your emotions as you express your gratitude to the Lord of the universe, the Babe in the manger, the Man on the cross.

Gratitude

_____

_____

_____

_____

_____

_____

_____

_____

10. Warren W. Wiersbe, *Real Worship* (Nashville, Tenn.: Thomas Nelson Publishers, Oliver-Nelson Books, 1986), p. 24.

Chapter 4

SINCE CHRIST HAS COME . . . WHAT'S HAPPENING?

Selected Scriptures

According to legend, in 1822 a certain father was traveling by sleigh to purchase a Christmas turkey when a fanciful poem began to stir in his mind. Returning home, he jotted down the verses and that night gathered his family around the fire. With wide-eyed wonder, his little ones delighted in his poetic description of St. Nicholas as a "right jolly old elf" who rode a magic sleigh heaped with toys and pulled by "eight tiny reindeer." Clement C. Moore's enchanting "The Night before Christmas" has since been retold countless times, becoming the inspiration for every child's Christmas sugarplum fantasies.

Almost two hundred Christmases and thousands of shopping trips later, another father has composed a somewhat less idealistic poem about the yuletide event. It is titled "'Twas the Day *after* Christmas."

> 'Twas the day after Christmas,
>   When all through the place
> There were arguments and depression—
>   Even Mom had a long face.
>
> The stockings hung empty,
>   And the house was a mess;
> The new clothes didn't fit . . .
>   And Dad was under stress.
>
> The family was irritable,
>   And the children—no one could please;
> Because the instructions for the swing set
>   Were written in Chinese!
>
> The bells no longer jingled,
>   And no carolers came around;
> The sink was stacked with dishes,
>   And the tree was turning brown.
>
> The stores were full of people
>   Returning things that fizzled and failed,

And the shoppers were discouraged
Because everything they'd bought was now on
half-price sale!

'Twas the day AFTER Christmas—
The spirit of joy had disappeared;
The only hope on the horizon
Was twelve bowl games the first day of the
New Year![1]

Before Christmas, we dream like children about Santa Claus and his glittering gifts of joy and peace. But after Christmas, the tinsel tarnishes, the tree dries up, and it's back to life as usual. With a sigh, we survey the tossed-aside toys, the stack of dirty dishes, and the even higher stack of unpaid bills; and pretty soon our "Ho ho ho!" turns to "Oh oh oh!"

Thankfully, though, the true hope of Christmas never fades or disappoints, because the days after that first Noel were filled with a wonder all their own.

History: A Brief Biblical Survey

To escape fantasy's buildup and inevitable letdown, let's take firm hold of our very real hope woven through those years following Christ's days in the manger.

Visit of the Magi

Matthew 2:1–12 recounts the Magi's starlit journey to find the Light of the World. When they get as far as Jerusalem, city of Israel's kings, they begin asking around.

"Where is He who has been born King of the Jews?
For we saw His star in the east, and have come to
worship Him." (v. 2)

Their inquiry rattles the Jews' present king, Herod, who immediately summons the top religious leaders to find the answer. They soon unearth Micah's prophecy pinpointing nearby Bethlehem. Herod furtively passes this on to the foreign worshipers, trusting that they'll find this new King and tell him where He is—so he

1. Charles R. Swindoll, "'Twas the Day *after* Christmas," from the sermon "Since Christ Has Come . . . What's Happening?" given at the First Evangelical Free Church of Fullerton, California, December 27, 1992.

can kill Him (vv. 3–8, 13).

Unaware of Herod's scheme, the reverent Magi resume their journey.

> And lo, the star, which they had seen in the east, went on before them, until it came and stood over where the Child was. And when they saw the star, they rejoiced exceedingly with great joy. And they came into the house and saw the Child with Mary His mother; and they fell down and worshiped Him; and opening their treasures they presented to Him gifts of gold and frankincense and myrrh.[2] (vv. 9–11)

Their precious time of adoration ends, however, when they are alerted in a dream to the dark desires in Herod's heart. Obediently, these stargazers take another route back home (v. 12).

Escape to Egypt

Also warned in a dream is Joseph, who is instructed:

> "Arise and take the Child and His mother, and flee to Egypt, and remain there until I tell you; for Herod is going to search for the Child to destroy Him." And he arose and took the Child and His mother by night, and departed for Egypt; and was there until the death of Herod, that what was spoken by the Lord through the prophet might be fulfilled, saying, "Out of Egypt did I call My Son." (vv. 13–15)

While Joseph, Mary, and young Jesus were escaping to safety, the rest of Bethlehem wasn't so fortunate. Herod, enraged that the Magi had foiled his plan, ruthlessly ordered the death of all boys ages two and under (v. 16).[3]

---

2. According to tradition, there were three Magi, each bearing a gift. But the Bible refers only to three gifts, so there could have been any number of Magi. Many commentators "have found symbolic value in the three gifts—gold suggesting royalty, incense divinity, and myrrh the Passion and burial." D. A. Carson, "Matthew," in *The Expositor's Bible Commentary*, ed. Frank E. Gaebelein (Grand Rapids, Mich.: Zondervan Publishing House, Regency Reference Library, 1984), vol. 8, p. 89.

3. Stepping back from this heart-wrenching scene, we can see plainly that Jesus was not still a "babe in a manger" when the Magi came but could have been as old as two. We can assume this because of Herod's decree concerning the murder of all the Bethlehem boys two years old and younger (v. 16). Also, Matthew consistently refers to Him as "the Child" (vv. 8, 9, 11, 13, 14, 20–21) rather than the "baby" (Luke 2:12).

Return to Nazareth

Far away from Herod's sting, Jesus remained hidden in Egypt until the murderous king died. Then, as promised, the angel revisited Joseph, saying:

> "Arise and take the Child and His mother, and go into the land of Israel; for those who sought the Child's life are dead." (v. 20)

Jesus and His family returned to the land of Israel, much like Moses and the Hebrews centuries earlier. The Judean region, however, was still dangerous; so Joseph, once more warned by God, took his family to calmer Galilee and settled down in the city where the angel had first visited Mary: Nazareth (vv. 21–23).

Growing-Up Years in Nazareth

Little is known of Jesus' days in Nazareth. The only gospel writer to open the door on Jesus' childhood is Luke, who just as quickly latches it again. Summing up Jesus' development, he writes:

> And the Child continued to grow and become strong, increasing in wisdom; and the grace of God was upon Him. (Luke 2:40)

Luke does give us one glimpse of Jesus' extraordinary wisdom, though, when He was only twelve years of age.

As a Boy in the Temple

That age was a significant year of transition for a young Jewish boy, because the next year, age thirteen, marked the entrance

> into the full responsibilities of adulthood. During the prior year the father was required to acquaint him with the duties and regulations which he was soon to assume.[4]

And where would Jesus go to be trained in His "duties and regulations"? To His Father's house, the temple, of course. So, after a family Passover journey to Jerusalem, Jesus lingered behind to learn in the temple . . . unbeknownst to Joseph and Mary. After

---

4. E. Earle Ellis, *The Gospel of Luke*, rev. ed., The New Century Bible Commentary series (1966; reprint, Grand Rapids, Mich.: William B. Eerdmans Publishing Co., 1974), p. 85.

a three-day search, his parents finally found Him

> sitting in the midst of the teachers, both listening to them, and asking them questions. And all who heard Him were amazed at His understanding and His answers. (vv. 46b–47)

When Mary saw Him, she scolded Him, but He replied, "Did you not know that I had to be in My Father's house?" (v. 49b). Although Mary and Joseph did not fully understand, Jesus at twelve already perceived His identity as God's Son and His divine mission.

Teenage and Young-Adult Years in Nazareth

Returning to Nazareth, Jesus spent the next eighteen years in obscurity, probably working alongside Joseph.[5] For many years, He was known simply as "the carpenter's son," until His baptism and the beginning of His ministry.

Baptism and Temptation in the Wilderness

In Mark 1, Jesus comes to the Jordan to be baptized by John; and as He emerges from the water, His true Father tells Him what He has known all along.

> "Thou art My beloved Son, in Thee I am well-pleased." (v. 11b, emphasis added)

With the Father's affirmation and the Spirit's descension as a dove, Jesus was commissioned for His messianic ministry. But first, "the Spirit impelled Him to go out into the wilderness," where Satan unsuccessfully tempted Him to bypass the Father's path to the Cross (vv. 12–13). Immediately afterward, He began His ministry, traveling and "preaching the gospel of God" (v. 14b).

His Three-and-a-Half-Year Ministry

Accompanying Him were the twelve disciples, with whom Jesus taught constantly, healed many, and gained a great following. At the same time, however, He raised the ire of the religious elite. Deploring their deadly legalism and empty ritualism, He preached a hopeful message of life, grace, and forgiveness.

---

5. Apparently, Joseph died before Jesus began His ministry, because from the cross, Jesus instructed John to take care of His mother (see John 19:26–27).

His Arrest, Trials, and Crucifixion

The more popular Jesus became, the more determined the religious leaders were to stop Him. Behind closed doors "they plotted together to seize Jesus by stealth, and kill Him" (Matt. 26:4).

Jesus knew of their scheming, yet He willingly surrendered Himself into their hands so that our redemption might be won through His sacrificial death. Arrested the night of Passover, He endured four spurious trials before the Jewish leaders and two trials before Pilate. At His final trial, exasperated by the shouts of the Jews, Pilate ordered Jesus to be crucified.

As He hung between heaven and earth, a small group of His followers gathered around the cross. Among them was His mother. "A sword will pierce even your own soul," old Simeon had told her when Jesus was a baby (Luke 2:35), and certainly her pain was great as she watched her precious Son suffer and die.

When He at last gasped, "It is finished" (John 19:30), all the prophecies about His birth, life, and death had been fulfilled. Joseph of Arimathea and Nicodemus took Jesus' body down, wrapped Him in linen cloths and spices, and buried Him in a nearby tomb (vv. 38–41).

His Bodily Resurrection

Three grief-filled days later, a piercing light broke through the despair when the disciples discovered His tomb was empty. Jesus was alive! For a few times more, they could touch Him and eat with Him—not as a ghost but as the resurrected Lord. Soon, however, He would leave earth and return permanently to heaven. His work here was done.

His Ascension

Gathering His disciples together one last time, He told them to wait for the Holy Spirit to empower them to be His witnesses to every nation (Acts 1:4–8). And then He was lifted into the sky until a cloud blocked Him from view. While the disciples were straining for another glimpse of Him,

> two men in white clothing stood beside them; and they also said, "Men of Galilee, why do you stand looking into the sky? This Jesus, who has been taken up from you into heaven, will come in just the same way as you have watched Him go into heaven." (vv. 10b–11)

Where He Is Now

Until Christ comes again in glory, Scripture teaches us that He is presently seated at the Father's

> right hand in the heavenly places, far above all rule and authority and power and dominion, and every name that is named, not only in this age, but also in the one to come. (Eph. 1:20b–21)

He is reigning over all the events in this world. Nothing escapes His notice or His careful control.

What He Is Doing

In His place of authority next to the Father, Jesus acts as our permanent High Priest. In this role,

> He is able to save forever those who draw near to God through Him, since He always lives to make intercession for them. (Heb. 7:25; see also Rom. 8:34)

Satan may accuse us when we sin, but Christ is there to plead our case: "we have an Advocate with the Father, Jesus Christ the righteous" (1 John 2:1). On the basis of His blood shed for us at Calvary, we stand cleansed and forgiven before God, awaiting the day when we will meet Him face-to-face.

Prophecy: A Quick Glimpse into the Future

Our great reunion day will come at the Rapture, when

> the Lord Himself will descend from heaven with a shout, with the voice of the archangel, and with the trumpet of God; and the dead in Christ shall rise first. Then we who are alive and remain shall be caught up together with them in the clouds to meet the Lord in the air, and thus we shall always be with the Lord. (1 Thess. 4:16–17)

The gentle Lamb of God who lay in Mary's arms and who hung limply on the cross will become the Lion of heaven—parting the clouds, calling His people home, and returning to earth as judge. *That* is the true story of Christmas. The Advent season is not just a commemoration of the past, it's a celebration for today and a hope for the future. Indeed, Christmas is a promise of salvation and glory we can cherish all year long.

Practicality: Some Timely Hints

Although it's the time to put away the ornaments, finish up the leftover turkey, and say good-bye to the relatives, after Christmas is also a time for reflection. It's a time to look back, look within, and look ahead.

Looking back at all the miracles surrounding Christ's first arrival— be real, be encouraged. Jesus Christ is no make-believe Santa Claus we hope will bring us happiness if we're good. Because He's real we can be real and encouraged that our lives are founded on solid truth.

Looking within at your personal walk with the Lord—be honest, be holy. How well are you relating to the Christ who came as a baby? How can you follow Him more devoutly?

Looking ahead—be aware, be ready. Be informed about how our times reflect prophecy. At any moment the clouds may part, the archangel may shout, and the trumpet may sound. At any moment we may find ourselves in the presence of our Lord, breathing the air of heaven and worshiping our King in joy and peace forever.

Now that's no sugarplum fantasy!

———◆———

Eternal Christmas

In the pure soul, although it sing or pray,
The Christ is born anew from day to day;
The life that knoweth Him shall bide apart
And keep eternal Christmas in the heart.[6]

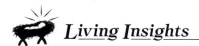 *Living Insights*   STUDY ONE

The flame from the oil lamp cast sleepy shadows on the wall as Mary pulled a blanket over Jesus. Finally, her little boy's chubby toddler legs were still and resting. His busy hands were folded close to His face. His lips were parted slightly, allowing steady breaths to

6. Elizabeth Stuart Phelps, "Eternal Christmas," in *Masterpieces of Religious Verse*, ed. James Dalton Morrison (New York, N.Y.: Harper and Brothers Publishers, 1948), no. 509.

pass in and out. Across the pillow lay His tousled hair, still curled from wind and play. Tenderly, she kissed his cheek and blew out the lamp.

"Mary, come look!" whispered Joseph urgently. Following him to the window, Mary peered through the curtain at a group of magnificent camels pawing up dust in front of the house. A tanned man in foreign dress called out a few orders. Another man pulled at the straps on his great beast, untying baggage. Servants rushed to their duties.

With questioning eyes, Mary glanced at her husband. In a moment there was a knock.

Cautiously opening the door, Joseph stood before the men and saw the dirt of hard travel on their cloaks and a nervous eagerness in their eyes. "We've come to see the child."

Lamps were lit, and Mary went to get Jesus. With His head on His mother's shoulder, the boy entered the room rubbing His eyes and yawning. The elegant strangers caught their breaths, as if Mary were showing them some rare emerald. Setting Him down, she stepped back and watched in amazement as the men bowed low and presented to Him their exquisite gifts.

They told Mary and Joseph how they had studied the Jewish prophecies about a mighty King from Judah, and they had searched the night skies for a sign of His appearing. Then, when they had seen the star, they determined to come worship this Ruler-God—no distance was too far, no cost too great. "This is no ordinary boy," they said to the parents, who nodded in agreement.

Just then, Jesus clapped his hands and grinned playfully. The royal Magi laughed with delight, gave one last bow, and left for home.

———◆———

The Magi teach us powerful lessons about loving Christ. They came for one reason, to worship the child, sacrificially and with a whole heart. They did not come seeking power or asking Jesus to grant them three wishes. Praise was their purpose.

So often we come to Jesus with our hands out, not as the Magi with faces bowed. We ask Him to give *us* gifts—gifts of health and happiness. How seldom do we offer Him our treasures.

In quietness, take a few moments for worship. Offer the Christ child your most precious gift of all: yourself. Give Him your love, your time, your hopes, your sorrows. Set them before Him in adoration. And watch for His gentle smile.

Adoration

_____

_____

_____

_____

_____

_____

_____

_____

Living Insights

In this four-chapter study of Christ, we've examined four questions:

- What was Jesus doing before He was born?

- Why did He come to earth?

- How could He as God become a man?

- Since He came, what has He been doing?

As a wrap-up to our study, take a few minutes to leaf through the guide and briefly summarize the answers to these questions. Then jot down one practical impact each answer makes on your life. In this way, we hope you leave this study knowing Christ better and carrying Christmas in your heart throughout the year.

Before the Son Became a Baby

Summary: _____

_____

_____

Application: _____

_____

_____

Why in Heaven Would God Come Down?

Summary: _____

_____

_____

Application: _____

_____

_____

The Gift Too Wonderful for Words

Summary: _____

_____

_____

Application: _____

_____

_____

Since Christ Has Come . . . What's Happening?

Summary: _____

_____

_____

Application: _____

_____

_____

BOOKS FOR
PROBING FURTHER

Christmastime is a feast for the senses. Take a deep breath—you can almost smell the apple-cinnamon wassail simmering on the stove. The warm sugar cookies right out of the oven. The freshly cut Christmas tree. Listen—you can almost hear the carols filling the house with the joyous sounds of the season.

Now's the time to draw a cozy sweater around your shoulders, bury your toes in a pair of snuggly slippers, and enjoy some family time around the fireplace. To borrow Charles Dickens' opening line from *A Tale of Two Cities*, Christmas is indeed "the best of times."

But it can be "the worst of times" too. Less than idyllic is the scene at the local mall—cars fighting for parking spots, shoppers shoving each other in line, kids screaming, tempers flaring. Then there are the holiday chores: clean the house, mail the Christmas cards, plan a party for the relatives, hang the decorations . . . the list never seems to end.

Christmas. The best of times, the worst of times; a time of peace, a time of turmoil.

To help you cope with the turmoil and increase the peace in your home, we've compiled the following list of resources. Some of these books relate directly to Christmas; others focus on Christ and the spiritual refreshment He can offer you any time of the year.

Chapin, Alice. *Great Christmas Ideas*. Wheaton, Ill.: Tyndale House Publishers, 1992.

Green, Michael. *Who Is This Jesus?* Nashville, Tenn.: Thomas Nelson Publishers, Oliver-Nelson Books, 1992.

Lucado, Max. *God Came Near*. Portland, Oreg.: Multnomah Press, 1987.

Minirth, Frank, Don Hawkins, and Paul Meier. *Happy Holidays: How to Beat the Holiday Blues*. Grand Rapids, Mich.: Baker Book House, 1990.

Tada, Joni Eareckson. *A Christmas Longing*. Portland, Oreg.: Multnomah Press, 1990.

All of the books listed are recommended reading; however, some may be out of print and available only through a library. For books currently available, please contact your local Christian bookstore. Works by Charles R. Swindoll are available through Insight for Living. IFL also offers some books by other authors—please note the Ordering Information that follows and contact the office that serves you.

ORDERING INFORMATION

JESUS: WHEN GOD BECAME A MAN

Cassette Tapes and Study Guide

This Bible study guide was designed to be used independently or in conjunction with the broadcast of Chuck Swindoll's taped messages which are listed below. If you would like to order cassette tapes or further copies of this study guide, please see the information given below and the order forms provided at the end of this guide.

		U.S.	Canada
JGM SG	Study guide	$ 3.95	$ 5.25
JGM CS	Cassette series, includes album cover	16.60	21.75
JGM 1–2	Individual cassettes, includes messages A and B	6.30	8.00

The prices are subject to change without notice.

JGM   1-A: *Before the Son Became a Baby*—John 1:1–18
        B: *Why in Heaven Would God Come Down?*— Selected Scriptures

JGM   2-A: *The Gift Too Wonderful for Words*—Philippians 2:5–8
        B: *Since Christ Has Come . . . What's Happening?*— Selected Scriptures

How to Order by Phone or FAX
(Credit card orders only)

United States: 1-800-772-8888 from 7:00 A.M. to 4:30 P.M., Pacific time, Monday through Friday
FAX (714) 575-5496 anytime, day or night

Canada: 1-800-663-7639, Vancouver residents call (604) 596-2910 from 7:00 A.M. to 5:00 P.M., Pacific time, Monday through Friday
FAX (604) 596-2975 anytime, day or night

Australia: (03) 872-4606 or FAX (03) 874-8890 from 9:00 A.M. to 5:00 P.M., Monday through Friday

Other International Locations: call the Ordering Services Department in the United States at (714) 575-5000 during the hours listed above.

How to Order by Mail

United States
- Mail to: Ordering Services Department
  Insight for Living
  Post Office Box 69000
  Anaheim, CA 92817-0900
- Sales tax: California residents add 7.25%.
- Shipping: add 10% of the total order amount for first-class delivery. (Otherwise, allow four to six weeks for fourth-class delivery.)
- Payment: personal checks, money orders, credit cards (Visa, MasterCard, Discover Card). No invoices or COD orders available.
- $10 fee for *any* returned check.

Canada
- Mail to: Insight for Living Ministries
  Post Office Box 2510
  Vancouver, BC V6B 3W7
- Sales tax: Please add 7% GST. British Columbia residents also add 7% sales tax (on tapes or cassette series).
- Shipping: included in prices listed above.
- Payment: personal checks, money orders, credit cards (Visa, Master-Card). No invoices or COD orders available.
- Delivery: approximately four weeks.

Australia, New Zealand, or Papua New Guinea
- Mail to: Insight for Living, Inc.
  GPO Box 2823 EE
  Melbourne, Victoria 3001, Australia
- Shipping and delivery time: please see chart that follows.
- Payment: personal checks payable in U.S. funds, international money orders, or credit cards (Visa, MasterCard).

Other International Locations
- Mail to: Ordering Services Department
  Insight for Living
  Post Office Box 69000
  Anaheim, CA 92817-0900
- Shipping and delivery time: please see chart that follows.
- Payment: personal checks payable in U.S. funds, international money orders, or credit cards (Visa, MasterCard).

Type of Shipping	Postage Cost	Delivery
Surface	10% of total order*	6 to 10 weeks
Airmail	25% of total order*	under 6 weeks

*Use U.S. price as a base.

Our Guarantee

Your complete satisfaction is our top priority here at Insight for Living. If you're not completely satisfied with anything you order, please return it for full credit, a refund, or a replacement, as *you* prefer.

Insight for Living Catalog

The Insight for Living catalog features study guides, tapes, and books by a variety of Christian authors. To obtain a free copy, call us at the numbers listed above.

Order Form
United States, Australia, and Overseas
(Canadian residents please use order form on reverse side.)

JGM CS represents the entire *Jesus: When God Became a Man* series in a special album cover, while JGM 1–2 are the individual tapes included in the series. JGM SG represents this study guide, should you desire to order additional copies.

JGM	SG	Study guide	$ 3.95
JGM	CS	Cassette series, includes album cover	16.60
JGM	1–2	Individual cassettes, includes messages A and B	6.30

Product Code	Product Description	Quantity	Unit Price	Total
			$	$
		Subtotal		
		California Residents—Sales Tax *Add 7.25% of subtotal.*		
		U.S. First-Class Shipping *For faster delivery, add 10% for postage and handling.*		
		Non-United States Residents *U.S. price plus 10% surface postage or 25% airmail.*		
		Gift to Insight for Living *Tax-deductible in the United States.*		
		Total Amount Due *Please do not send cash.*	$	

Prices are subject to change without notice.

Payment by: ❏ Check or money order payable to Insight for Living   ❏ Credit card

(Circle one): Visa   MasterCard   Discover Card   Number _____

Expiration Date _____   Signature _____
We cannot process your credit card purchase without your signature.

Name _____

Address _____

City _____   State _____

Zip Code _____   Country _____

Telephone (____) _____   Radio Station ____ ____ ____ ____
If questions arise concerning your order, we may need to contact you.

Mail this order form to the Ordering Services Department at one of these addresses:

Insight for Living
Post Office Box 69000, Anaheim, CA 92817-0900

Insight for Living, Inc.
GPO Box 2823 EE, Melbourne, VIC 3001, Australia

Order Form
Canadian Residents

(Residents of the United States, Australia, and other international locations, please use order form on reverse side.)

JGM CS represents the entire *Jesus: When God Became a Man* series in a special album cover, while JGM 1–2 are the individual tapes included in the series. JGM SG represents this study guide, should you desire to order additional copies.

JGM	SG	Study guide	$ 5.25
JGM	CS	Cassette series, includes album cover	21.75
JGM	1–2	Individual cassettes, includes messages A and B	8.00

Product Code	Product Description	Quantity	Unit Price	Total
			$	$
		Subtotal		
		Add 7% GST		
		British Columbia Residents *Add 7% sales tax on individual tapes or cassette series.*		
		Gift to Insight for Living Ministries *Tax-deductible in Canada.*		
		Total Amount Due *Please do not send cash.*		$

Prices are subject to change without notice.

Payment by: ❑ Check or money order payable to Insight for Living Ministries
❑ Credit card

(Circle one): Visa   MasterCard   Number _____

Expiration Date_____   Signature_____
We cannot process your credit card purchase without your signature.

Name_____

Address_____

City_____   Province_____

Postal Code_____   Country_____

Telephone (_____)_____   Radio Station____ ____ ____ ____
If questions arise concerning your order, we may need to contact you.

Mail this order form to the Ordering Services Department at the following address:

Insight for Living Ministries
Post Office Box 2510
Vancouver, BC, Canada V6B 3W7

Order Form
United States, Australia, and Overseas

(Canadian residents please use order form on reverse side.)

JGM CS represents the entire *Jesus: When God Became a Man* series in a special album cover, while JGM 1–2 are the individual tapes included in the series. JGM SG represents this study guide, should you desire to order additional copies.

JGM	SG	Study guide	$ 3.95
JGM	CS	Cassette series, includes album cover	16.60
JGM	1–2	Individual cassettes, includes messages A and B	6.30

Product Code	Product Description	Quantity	Unit Price	Total
			$	$
		Subtotal		
		California Residents—Sales Tax Add 7.25% of subtotal.		
		U.S. First-Class Shipping For faster delivery, add 10% for postage and handling.		
		Non-United States Residents U.S. price plus 10% surface postage or 25% airmail.		
		Gift to Insight for Living Tax-deductible in the United States.		
		Total Amount Due Please do not send cash.	$	

Prices are subject to change without notice.

Payment by: ❑ Check or money order payable to Insight for Living   ❑ Credit card

(Circle one): Visa   MasterCard   Discover Card   Number _____

Expiration Date _____   Signature _____
We cannot process your credit card purchase without your signature.

Name _____

Address _____

City _____   State _____

Zip Code _____   Country _____

Telephone (___) _____   Radio Station ____ ____ ____ ____
If questions arise concerning your order, we may need to contact you.

Mail this order form to the Ordering Services Department at one of these addresses:

Insight for Living
Post Office Box 69000, Anaheim, CA 92817-0900

Insight for Living, Inc.
GPO Box 2823 EE, Melbourne, VIC 3001, Australia

Order Form
Canadian Residents

(Residents of the United States, Australia, and other international locations, please use order form on reverse side.)

JGM CS represents the entire *Jesus: When God Became a Man* series in a special album cover, while JGM 1–2 are the individual tapes included in the series. JGM SG represents this study guide, should you desire to order additional copies.

JGM	SG	Study guide	$ 5.25
JGM	CS	Cassette series, includes album cover	21.75
JGM	1–2	Individual cassettes, includes messages A and B	8.00

Product Code	Product Description	Quantity	Unit Price	Total
			$	$
		Subtotal		
		Add 7% GST		
		British Columbia Residents *Add 7% sales tax on individual tapes or cassette series.*		
		Gift to Insight for Living Ministries *Tax-deductible in Canada.*		
		Total Amount Due *Please do not send cash.*	$	

Prices are subject to change without notice.

Payment by: ❑ Check or money order payable to Insight for Living Ministries
❑ Credit card

(Circle one): Visa   MasterCard   Number _____

Expiration Date _____   Signature _____
We cannot process your credit card purchase without your signature.

Name _____

Address _____

City _____   Province _____

Postal Code _____   Country _____

Telephone (___) _____   Radio Station ____ ____ ____ ____
If questions arise concerning your order, we may need to contact you.

Mail this order form to the Ordering Services Department at the following address:

Insight for Living Ministries
Post Office Box 2510
Vancouver, BC, Canada V6B 3W7

Order Form
United States, Australia, and Overseas
(Canadian residents please use order form on reverse side.)

JGM CS represents the entire *Jesus: When God Became a Man* series in a special album cover, while JGM 1–2 are the individual tapes included in the series. JGM SG represents this study guide, should you desire to order additional copies.

JGM	SG	Study guide	$ 3.95
JGM	CS	Cassette series, includes album cover	16.60
JGM	1–2	Individual cassettes, includes messages A and B	6.30

Product Code	Product Description	Quantity	Unit Price	Total
			$	$
		Subtotal		
	California Residents—Sales Tax *Add 7.25% of subtotal.*			
	U.S. First-Class Shipping *For faster delivery, add 10% for postage and handling.*			
	Non-United States Residents *U.S. price plus 10% surface postage or 25% airmail.*			
	Gift to Insight for Living *Tax-deductible in the United States.*			
	Total Amount Due *Please do not send cash.*		$	

Prices are subject to change without notice.

Payment by: ❑ Check or money order payable to Insight for Living   ❑ Credit card

(Circle one): Visa   MasterCard   Discover Card   Number _____

Expiration Date _____   Signature _____
We cannot process your credit card purchase without your signature.

Name _____

Address _____

City _____   State _____

Zip Code _____   Country _____

Telephone (____) _____   Radio Station ____ ____ ____ ____
If questions arise concerning your order, we may need to contact you.

Mail this order form to the Ordering Services Department at one of these addresses:

Insight for Living
Post Office Box 69000, Anaheim, CA 92817-0900

Insight for Living, Inc.
GPO Box 2823 EE, Melbourne, VIC 3001, Australia

Order Form
Canadian Residents

(Residents of the United States, Australia, and other international locations, please use order form on reverse side.)

JGM CS represents the entire *Jesus: When God Became a Man* series in a special album cover, while JGM 1–2 are the individual tapes included in the series. JGM SG represents this study guide, should you desire to order additional copies.

JGM	SG	Study guide	$ 5.25
JGM	CS	Cassette series, includes album cover	21.75
JGM	1–2	Individual cassettes, includes messages A and B	8.00

Product Code	Product Description	Quantity	Unit Price	Total
			$	$
	Subtotal			
	Add 7% GST			
	British Columbia Residents *Add 7% sales tax on individual tapes or cassette series.*			
	Gift to Insight for Living Ministries *Tax-deductible in Canada.*			
	Total Amount Due *Please do not send cash.*		$	

Prices are subject to change without notice.

Payment by: ❏ Check or money order payable to Insight for Living Ministries
❏ Credit card

(Circle one): Visa   MasterCard   Number _____

Expiration Date_____   Signature_____
We cannot process your credit card purchase without your signature.

Name_____

Address_____

City_____   Province_____

Postal Code_____   Country_____

Telephone (_____) _____   Radio Station____ ____ ____ ____
If questions arise concerning your order, we may need to contact you.

Mail this order form to the Ordering Services Department at the following address:

Insight for Living Ministries
Post Office Box 2510
Vancouver, BC, Canada V6B 3W7